SAVOR LIFE
a delicious way to grow!

Author Nataliia Prokopchik
Illustrator Anastasiia Zhelik

by NataWithKids
Las Vegas, Nevada, USA

Author
Nataliia Prokopchik

Savor Life: A Delicious Way to Grow
Spring — Book 2
of the Savor Life Series

© 2025 NataWithKids LLC. All rights reserved.
No part of this book may be reproduced or transmitted in any form or by any means, electronic or mechanical, including photocopying, recording, or any information storage or retrieval system, without the prior written permission of the publisher, except in the case of brief quotations used in reviews or critical articles.
All recipes, stories, questions, activities, and other original texts
© Nataliia Prokopchik.

ISBN: 978-1-971721-01-9
Library of Congress Control Number: 2026902658

First edition, February 2026
Printed in the United States of America

Illustrations and cover design by Anastasiia Zhelik

Interior layout by Alexander Dubasov

Published by NataWithKids LLC

Las Vegas, Nevada

www.natawithkids.com

THIS BOOK BELONGS TO

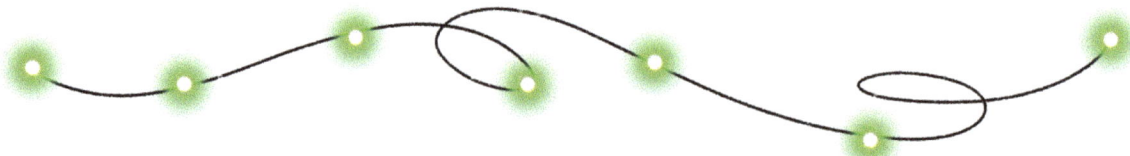

Dedicated to all adults who recognize the value
of cooking together with children and see it not only the joy
of creating and a delicious results, but also fertile ground for nurturing
essential life skills and strong character in little ones.

May every recipe you experience together become a step toward inner
growth — for both adult and child.

To Nathaniel Chirva — just beginning his journey.
May you grow surrounded by love and discover the world with joy.
With love.

Table of Contents

Carrot-Apple Muffins 10

Blooming Almond Shortbread Cookies 12

Vanilla Cupcakes 16

Chocolate Cupcakes 17

Bird's Nest Cupcake Toppers 19

Crackers 24

Chocolate Chia Pudding 30

Chocolate Cake (Layer) 31

Little Sprout Dessert Cups 32

Mini Pies 40

Vanilla and Chocolate Cookies 46

Spring Meadow Pizza 52

Spring Bird Cookies 58

Banana Chocolate Cookies 60

Pancakes 68

Mango Loaf Cake 70

Puff Pastry Carrots 72

Spring Salad 75

Flaxseed Bread 78

Waffle Sandwich 79

Bunny Sandwich 80

🌟 And beyond the recipes... discover more than 45 additional illustrated pages with riddles, conversation starters, thought-provoking questions, mazes, and other creative activities.

🌟 Special pages for parents featuring reflections on parenting and growing together.

Daddy Bear, Mommy Bear, Lily, and Toby spent a wonderful winter together. It was filled with cozy traditions, the joy of cooking treats side by side, and happy memories they will treasure as their greatest gift.

With gratitude and great curiosity, the bear family now steps into a new season. They are ready to welcome spring.
Let's go together toward new discoveries.

Let's see what we need to make spring treats together.

I help you measure just the right amount.
With me, you always know how much to add.
Your recipe turns out just right every time.
What am I?

MEASURING CUPS AND SPOONS

blender

waffle maker

piping bag

muffin pans

cupcake liners

loaf pan

I help you cook pancakes, eggs, and cutlets.
I make food golden and crispy.
Together with the stove, I help make everything delicious.
What am I?

FRYING PAN

square baking pan

parchment paper

baking tray

hand grinder

cookie cutters

frying pan

9

Carrot-Apple Muffins

Ingredients (Makes 12 muffins):

- 1 cup grated carrot (about 2 medium carrots)
- 1 cup grated apple (about 1 medium apple)
- 1 + 1/2 cups whole wheat flour
- 1 + 1/2 teaspoons baking powder
- 1/2 teaspoon baking soda
- 1/4 teaspoon salt
- 1/2 cup chopped nuts (optional)
- 2 eggs
- 1/2 cup vegetable oil
- 1/2 cup honey or maple syrup
- 1/4 cup milk

Creative Process

1. Wash, peel, and grate the carrots and apple.
2. Preheat the oven to 350°F (180°C).
3. Grease a muffin tin or line it with paper liners.
4. In one bowl, mix all the dry ingredients.
5. In another bowl, lightly beat the eggs. Add the oil, honey or maple syrup, and milk. Mix well. Then gradually add the flour mixture. Stir until combined. Add the grated carrots and apple. Mix again.
6. Fill each muffin cup about two-thirds full, leaving room for the muffins to rise.
7. Bake for 20 to 25 minutes, or until a toothpick inserted into the center comes out clean.
8. Remove from the oven and let cool.

Enjoy!

Blooming Almond Shortbread Cookies

Ingredients:
- 1/2 cup softened butter
- 1/3 cup sugar
- 1 egg yolk
- 1 teaspoon vanilla extract
- 1/4 teaspoon salt
- 1 + 1/2 + 1/4 cups (180 g) almond flour
- 1 tablespoon coconut flour
- 1/2 teaspoon baking powder
- jam (for filling)

Creative Process

1. Using a mixer, beat the softened butter and sugar for 2 to 3 minutes until light and creamy.

2. Add the egg yolk, vanilla extract, and salt. Beat again until well combined.

3. In a separate bowl, mix the almond flour, coconut flour, and baking powder.

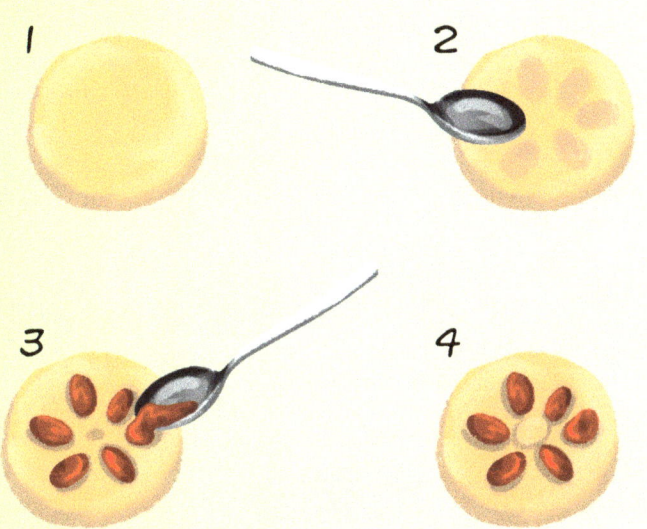

4. Add the dry mixture to the butter mixture. Mix until a soft dough forms.

5. Shape the dough into small balls and place them on a baking sheet lined with parchment paper.

6. Gently flatten each ball. Use your finger or a spoon to make small petal-shaped indentations. Fill them with jam.

7. Chill the cookies in the refrigerator for 15 minutes to help them hold their shape.

8. Preheat the oven to 350°F (175°C).

9. Bake for 10 to 12 minutes, until the edges turn golden.

Enjoy!

Let's notice how nature wakes up in spring.

Snow is melting.
Streams are flowing.
Birds are singing.
The forest is waking up.

What flowers can you find?
Why is it important to leave them where they grow?
How can we help keep nature clean and safe?

Vanilla Cupcakes

Ingredients (Makes 12 cupcakes):

- 180 g all-purpose flour
- 1 + 1/2 teaspoons baking powder
- a pinch of salt
- 120 g softened butter
- 120 g sugar
- 2 eggs
- 120 ml milk
- 1 to 2 teaspoons vanilla extract

Creative Process

1. Preheat the oven to 338°F (170°C).
2. In a small bowl, sift the flour. Add the baking powder and salt. Mix well and set aside.
3. In a large bowl, beat the softened butter and sugar until light and fluffy. This takes about 2 to 3 minutes.
4. Add the eggs one at a time, beating well after each addition. Stir in the vanilla extract.
5. Using a spatula, gently fold in the flour mixture and milk, alternating between them, until all ingredients are combined.
6. Fill the cupcake cups about two-thirds full.
7. Bake for 18 to 22 minutes.
8. Remove from the oven and let cool.

Enjoy!

Chocolate Cupcakes

Ingredients (Makes 16 cupcakes):
- 180 g all-purpose flour
- 50 g cocoa powder
- 2 teaspoons baking powder
- a pinch of salt
- 2 eggs
- 200 g sugar
- 180 ml milk
- 120 g melted butter
- 1 teaspoon vanilla extract

Creative Process

1. Preheat the oven to 347°F (175°C).
2. In a small bowl, mix the cocoa powder, flour, salt, and baking powder. Set aside.
3. In a large bowl, beat the eggs with the sugar and vanilla until light and smooth.
4. Add the milk and melted butter. Mix well.
5. Gradually add the dry ingredients. Stir until smooth.
6. Fill the cupcake cups about two-thirds full.
7. Bake for 18 to 20 minutes.
8. Remove from the oven and let cool.

Enjoy!

In spring, birds build nests, lay eggs, and care for their babies.

Watching busy little birds inspired the bear cubs to decorate their favorite cupcakes in a special way.

Bird's Nest Cupcake Toppers

Cream Ingredients:

- 1/2 cup cold heavy cream
- 1 to 2 tablespoons cocoa powder
- 1 tablespoon powdered sugar
- 1 to 2 tablespoons cream cheese

Let the cupcakes cool completely before decorating. This will help the cream hold its shape.

Creative Process

1. Whip the cream until soft and fluffy.
2. Add the cocoa powder and cream cheese. Beat for another minute, until the cream holds its shape.
3. Fill a piping bag fitted with a grass tip. Pipe the cream in a circle on top of each cupcake to form a nest.
4. Make a small indentation in the center. Place chocolate eggs or little birds made of fondant or marzipan inside.

Enjoy!

Lily and Toby are making cupcakes.
Find the matching actions on both sides. Use both hands!

Left Hand

chop

pour

whisk

crack an egg

sift

pour

stir

Right Hand

sift

stir

pour

whisk

crack an egg

chop

pour

With Both Hands

fill

bake

decorate

Our bodies are a true miracle.
They help us experience the world.
    To taste.
    To smell.
    To see.
    To hear.
    To touch.
Each feeling is a gift from Heaven.

Look around.
What do you see?
What do you hear?

Taste slowly.
Breathe in the aroma.
Eat with gratitude.
Enjoy every moment.

Look closely.
Which cupcakes did Lily and Toby decorate the same way?
Which cupcake would you choose for yourself? Which one would you share?

Have you noticed the bees this spring?
Have you heard them buzzing?
Which bee will bring nectar back to the hive?

Crackers

Base Ingredients:

- 1/2 cup ground flaxseed (flax flour)
- 4 tablespoons chia seeds
- 1/4 cup hemp seeds
- (can be replaced with sesame seeds or poppy seeds)
- 1/4 cup sunflower seeds
- 1/4 cup pumpkin seeds
- 1/4 cup sesame seeds
- 1/2 cup quick oats (or almond flour)

For Savory Crackers:

- 2 teaspoons oregano
- 1 teaspoon ground cumin
- 1/2 teaspoon garlic powder
- 1/2 teaspoon salt
- 1 + 1/4 cups water

For Sweet Crackers:

- 1 + 1/4 cups water
- 1/4 cup honey or maple syrup
- 1/4 cup chopped dried cranberries or raisins

Creative Process

1 In a large bowl, measure and mix all the base ingredients and the dry ingredients for one flavor of your choice.

2 Add the water (and honey or syrup for sweet crackers). Mix well.

3 Let the mixture rest for 10 minutes.

4 Preheat the oven to 350°F (180°C).

5 Cut baking paper to fit your baking tray. Roll the dough out thinly and cut it into small pieces.

6 Bake until golden, about 20–30 minutes (depending on how thin the dough is).

Enjoy!

Microgreens are little plants that grow from seeds before they become big vegetables.

If you plant the same seeds in the garden, in the soil, at the right depth and spacing, they will grow into full vegetables and leafy greens.

These little plants are very good for your health and also add bright color and delicious flavor to your meals.

Radish microgreens have a spicy taste similar to regular radishes, but much milder. They are a wonderful addition to salads and sandwiches.

Pea microgreens have a sweet, delicate flavor. They make a healthy and beautiful garnish for soups and salads.

Basil microgreens have a fresh, aromatic taste, similar to regular basil but more delicate. They are perfect for dishes, spreads, and salads.

Growing microgreens is easy!

To get started, you will need:
- special seeds;
- a container with a lid;
- cotton pads or paper towels;
- water and light.

How to Grow Microgreens?

1 Line the container and gently moisten the surface. Spread the seeds evenly in one layer.

2 Lightly spray with water and cover with the lid.

3 After one day, remove the lid and place the container on a sunny windowsill.

4 Spray the seeds lightly every day so they do not dry out.

5 In 3–5 days, the first sprouts will appear.

6 When the plants reach 2–3 inches (5–7 cm), carefully cut them with scissors (we don't eat the roots!). Add them to your meals and enjoy something healthy and delicious.

A tiny seed sprouts and grows.
With warm rain and sunshine,
it becomes stronger each day
and reaches up toward the light,
slowly turning green.

Inside each of us, there are tiny seeds of kindness, courage, patience,
and not giving up and trying again and again.
These can also be our skills, like learning to cook or ride a bike.
Everything needs time to grow.
These «little seeds» grow when we care for them and give them attention.
Is there something you are learning right now?
Something small that is just beginning?
What can you do better today than yesterday?

Chocolate Chia Pudding

Ingredients:

- 3 tablespoons chia seeds
- 1 cup plant milk
- 1 tablespoon cocoa powder
- 1 to 2 teaspoons honey or maple syrup

Creative Process

1. In a bowl, mix the milk, cocoa powder, and honey until smooth.
2. Add the chia seeds and stir well.
3. Pour the mixture into small jars, cover with lids, and place in the refrigerator for 3–4 hours or overnight.

Enjoy!

Chocolate Cake (Layer)

Ingredients:

- 1 cup almond flour
- 1/4 cup cocoa powder
- 1 teaspoon baking powder
- 3 eggs
- 1/3 cup melted butter or coconut oil
- 1/4 cup honey
- 1/2 teaspoon vanilla extract
- 2 to 3 tablespoons coconut milk or almond milk

Creative Process

1. Preheat the oven to 350°F (180°C).
2. Grease a small baking pan or line it with parchment paper.
3. In one bowl, mix the dry ingredients.

4. In another bowl, whisk the wet ingredients.
5. Gradually add the dry mixture to the wet mixture, stirring until smooth.
6. Pour the batter into the pan and bake for 20–25 minutes.

Enjoy!

Little Sprout Dessert Cups

Ingredients:

- chia pudding
- chocolate cake layer
- decorations

Decoration Options:

1. a small bunch of fresh mint
2. fondant, chocolate, and a cracker stick
3. a strawberry and orange glaze

Creative Process

1. Fill small jars halfway (or a little more) with chia pudding.
2. Crumble the cooled chocolate cake layer and add it on top of the pudding.

3 Decorate your dessert using one or more of the options below.

- **Option 1**: Pinch off a few mint leaves, wash them, and «plant» them in the chocolate «soil.».

- **Option 2**: Shape small vegetables or berries from fondant. Cover a cracker stick with melted chocolate and attach the fondant decoration to it. Place it in the center of the dessert. (You can also make a tiny sprout and place it in the middle.)

- **Option 3**: Wash a strawberry, let it dry, then dip it in melted glaze. When the glaze sets, place your «carrot» in the center of the jar.

Decide for yourself what you would like to «plant» in your little garden 🙂

Enjoy!

Nature teaches us that everything grows step by step.
Everything takes time.
Look at how the flowers grow. Put the pictures in order and tell the story.

Take turns finding matching pairs (one item has no match).
Place a stone or token on both matching pictures.

We are more than just our bodies.
Our inner world needs care too.

It's a peaceful spring evening in the Bear Family's yard.
Imagine stepping inside.
Where would you go?
How would this evening make you feel?
What would you like to bring with you from it?

Mini Pies

Ingredients:
- 225 g whole wheat flour
- 50 g powdered sugar
- 1/2 teaspoon baking powder
- 100 g cold butter
- 1 egg
- 1–2 tablespoons cold water
- jam (for filling)

Creative Process

1. Sift the flour, baking powder, and powdered sugar into a bowl. Mix well.
2. Add the cold butter, cut into small cubes, and rub it into the dry ingredients until crumbly.
3. Add the egg and water. Mix to form a soft dough.
4. Preheat the oven to 400°F (200°C). 
5. Roll out the dough, cut out flower shapes, and place them into a muffin pan.
6. Gently press the centers with a small measuring spoon and fill with jam.
7. Bake for 13–20 minutes, until lightly golden.

Enjoy!

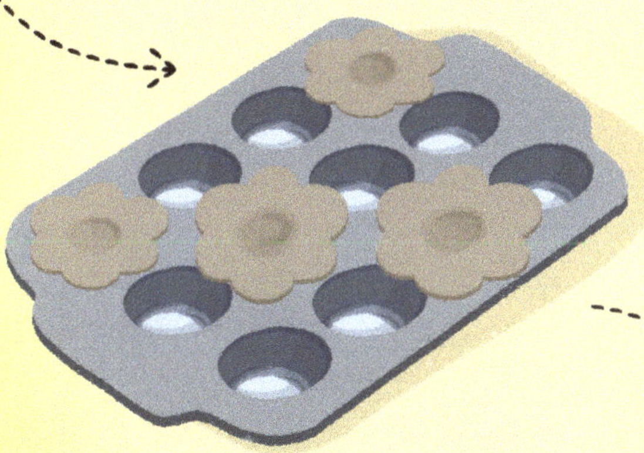

Look carefully at the picture and help the bears clean up.
Find what doesn't belong in the kitchen.
How does it feel to cook when everything is in its place?

On the farm, Lily and Toby learn where milk, butter, sour cream, cheese, and yogurt come from.

They see how much care, patience, love and hard work it takes to bring these foods to our table.

Which dairy food do you like the most?

Let's make a riddle together!

Choose one food and describe it out loud.
Start your riddle like this:
- I am made from…
- I taste like…
- I feel like…
- I am used for…

When you are ready, ask:
Can you guess what I am?

Vanilla and Chocolate Cookies

Ingredients:

- 1 cup sugar
- 1 cup soft butter (227 g)
- 2 eggs
- 3 cups flour
- 1/2 teaspoon baking powder
- 1/2 teaspoon vanilla extract (for the vanilla dough)
- 2-3 tablespoons cocoa powder (for the chocolate dough)

Creative Process

1. In a large bowl, beat the butter with the sugar. Add the eggs and mix well. Divide the mixture into two parts.

2. For the vanilla dough, add the vanilla extract, half the flour, and baking powder.

3. For the chocolate dough, add the cocoa powder and remaining flour and baking powder.

4. Knead both doughs, wrap them in plastic wrap, and chill in the refrigerator for 30 minutes.

5. Preheat the oven to 375°F (190°C).

6. Divide the dough into small pieces, roll them into balls, and shape them into little sheep (as shown in the picture).

7. Bake for about 15 minutes, until golden.

Enjoy!

From time to time, it's important to slow down and notice the beauty around us. To notice spring. To enjoy the rain, rainbows, new leaves, birds' songs, and blooming trees filled with sweet fragrance...

At the market, Mommy Bear and Daddy Bear choose ingredients for their family.
Mommy Bear reads the labels and thinks carefully before buying.
They know that cooking at home helps them choose what goes into their food.
Cooking is not just about food. It is about care, time, and love.

Let's think about it together.

- What is Mommy Bear looking at on the label?
- How can we tell if food is fresh?
- What can we learn from reading the label?

If you were with them, what would you pick first? Why?

Spring Meadow Pizza

Ingredients for the Dough:
- 1 + 1/2 cups almond flour
- 1 teaspoon baking powder
- 1/2 teaspoon salt
- 1 egg
- 1 cup shredded mozzarella cheese
- 1 tablespoon olive oil

Topping Ingredients:
- mini mozzarella balls
- orange cherry tomatoes
- fresh basil leaves
- ketchup
- favorite microgreens

Creative Process

1. Preheat the oven to 350°F (180°C).
2. In a small bowl, mix the almond flour, baking powder, and salt.
3. In a deep microwave-safe (non-metal) bowl, shred the mozzarella and melt it in the microwave until soft (about 20–30 seconds).
4. Add the olive oil, egg, and flour mixture to the cheese. Mix to form a dough.
5. Place the dough between two sheets of parchment paper and roll it into a thin circle.
6. Bake for 8–10 minutes, until lightly golden.
7. Carefully remove from the oven, spread with ketchup, and add the toppings.
8. Bake for another 5–7 minutes. Decorate with basil and microgreens.

Enjoy!

Lily and Toby welcome Grandma and Grandpa for a visit.

Can you find 10 differences between the two pictures?

Spring Bird Cookies

Ingredients:
- 1 cup kefir or yogurt
- 1/2 teaspoon baking soda
- 1/2 teaspoon salt
- 1–2 tablespoons sugar
- 1 egg
- 2 tablespoons oil
- 2 + 1/2–3 cups flour
- 1 egg (for brushing)
- raisins

This dough is also good for stuffed buns and pizza (just reduce the amount of sugar).

Creative Process

1. In a deep bowl, mix the kefir and baking soda. Let it rest for 2–3 minutes.
2. Add salt, sugar, egg, and oil. Whisk lightly.
3. Gradually sift in the flour and mix with a spoon. Then knead the dough with your hands.
4. The dough should be soft, but not sticky.
5. Let it rest for 15 minutes.
6. Preheat the oven to 180°C (350°F).
7. Shape little «birds.»
8. Start with a small rope of dough and tie it into a knot.
9. Then form the beak, add raisins for the eyes, and make the tail by pressing with a fork.
10. Brush with lightly beaten egg and bake for 20–25 minutes, until golden.

Enjoy!

Banana Chocolate Cookies

Ingredients:

- 1 ripe banana
- about 2 cups whole wheat flour
- 2 tablespoons cocoa powder
- 1/2 teaspoon baking soda
- a pinch of salt
- 1/2 cup butter (113 g)
- 1/4 cup honey or maple syrup
- chocolate glaze and fondant for decoration

Creative Process

1. Peel the banana and mash it into a puree.
2. Sift the flour into a large bowl. Add cocoa powder, baking soda, and salt. Mix well.
3. Cut the cold butter into small cubes and rub it into the flour mixture until crumbly.
4. Add the banana puree and honey. Mix the dough, wrap it in plastic wrap, and refrigerate for 30 minutes.

5. Preheat the oven to 350°F (180°C).
6. Lightly dust the board with flour and roll out the dough. Cut out flowers and leaves and place them on a baking sheet lined with parchment paper.
7. Bake for 10–12 minutes. Let cool and decorate.
8. Decorate the cookies with melted chocolate icing and sprinkles or fondant.
9. Use melted chocolate to «glue» the cookies to a wooden stick. Let them set.
10. Arrange the flowers into a bouquet and give it to Mom.

Find four matching pairs of cups.

Let's learn how to fold a napkin into a leaf and decorate the festive table.

1 Open the napkin and turn it so it looks like a diamond. Fold it in half.

2 Fold the triangle like an accordion, then fold it in half.

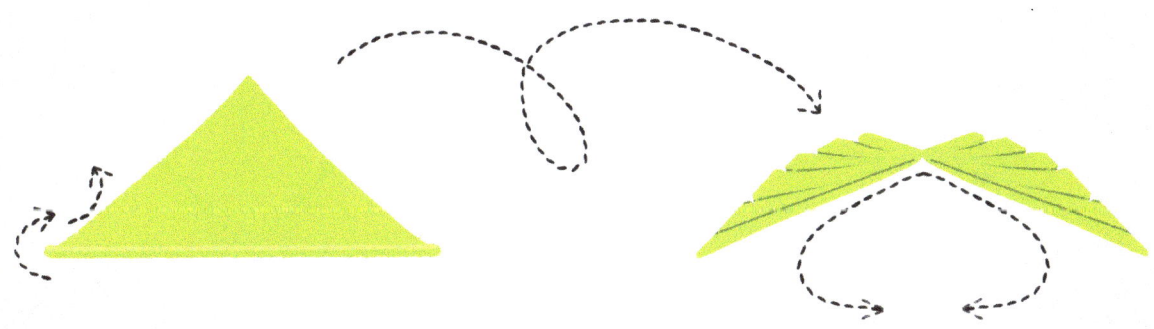

3 Clip the ends together to keep them in place.

Here is one of Lily and Toby's spring days.
How is it like yours?

Let's look at the picture and find the correct shadow.

Pancakes

Ingredients:

- 1 ripe banana (or 2 tablespoons applesauce)
- 2 eggs
- 1/2 cup milk
- 1/2 cup oat flour (or ground rolled oats)
- 1/2 cup vanilla protein powder
- 1/2 teaspoon baking powder
- a pinch of salt

Creative Process

1. In a blender, blend the banana (or applesauce), eggs, and milk until smooth.

2. Add the oat flour, protein powder, baking powder, and salt. Mix well.

3. Heat a pan over medium heat and lightly grease it with oil.

4. Pour small portions of batter onto the pan. Cook for 1–2 minutes, until bubbles appear. Flip and cook for another minute.

5. Top with berries and fruit pieces.

Enjoy!

FUN FACT:

LIONS SLEEP UP TO 20 HOURS A DAY, AND JUST LIKE YOU, THEY MIGHT EVEN DREAM WHILE THEY NAP!

I'm not just a king—I lead the way,
I help my friends, every day.

A leader is kind, strong, and true,
So That means, you're a leader too!

we had so much fun, we must now go,
Wave goodbye, to my friend Leo!

FUN FACT:

LIONS GREET EACH OTHER BY RUBBING HEADS—IT'S THEIR WAY OF SHOWING LOVE AND FRIENDSHIP!

www.ingramcontent.com/pod-product-compliance
Lightning Source LLC
LaVergne TN
LVRC081131100526
838202LV00075B/2844